ashley howell bunn

Books may be purchased in quantity and/or special sales by contacting the publisher. All inquiries related to such matters should be addressed to:

South Broadway Press LLC
1350 Josephine St Unit 102
Denver CO 80206

southbroadwaypress@gmail.com
www.southbroadwaypress.org

303.330.8083

First Paperback Edition, 2025
ISBN: 978-1-7350355-5-0
Library of Congress Control Number: 2026931183

Edited by: Tyler Hurula and Brice Maiurro

Front Cover Design: Ashley Howell Bunn, Brice Maiurro

Author Image:
© Marissa Morrow
Printed in the United States

praise for burning, breaking, building

"Through mirrors of grit and gratefulness, the poems in *burning, breaking, building* show us rock bottom within the framework of The Death Card in Tarot: both in the world of the dying and the living. Sometimes so tender it stings, Bunn has shed her skin on paper for us to smooth, a living legacy that will surely reclaim us, all of us, suffering the fate of desperation and despair. Let your body want, and know it is good. 'Let that soft animal love.'"

–Hillary Leftwich, Author of *Saint Dymphna's Playbook*

"A child believes he once existed as grass. A daughter recognizes the premonition in a sweater later knotted with grief. And sickness awakens a body memory of the hard paddle away from the island of drink. There is entanglement here, between recovery while mothering while mourning while wondering how a legacy is inherited or broken.

Ashley's words are strung and restrung, held lovingly, then soon scattered and gorgeously distilled as haibun passageways via erasure. Her stories stack thickly amongst fire, hospitals, snow, blood, and stars, until sheer deluge splits the body open and clarity surfaces amid a breath of sparsity whittled out of the fervid tendency to continue and continue.

Ashley Howell Bunn is unflinchingly fragile and embodied in this cyclical voyage with birth and death as her shipmates. With both pluck and wonder, she's showing us how it may be done."

—Jessica Rigney, Author of *Something Whole*

"When you find yourself lying prone, open up *burning, breaking, building* and slip into a cocoon of blackouts, tangled knots, and mourning moons. Like celestial bodies conceive the energy of the subterranean, pour yourself into the earth. Ashley Howell Bunn proves writer mothers do it best."

—Alexandra Naughton, Author of *Sick of Being Inside Myself*

"For of course a body, a home, a country, a heart — everything —must first burn for it to be rebuilt in its best image. It is the sacred work of the poet to scavenge through the ashes of all that was, and find within them some boiled down truth that will be the spirit of tomorrow, an elegy for the past, a potent echo of the now. In these pages, Ashley Howell Bunn does just this, showing us the still smoking, smoldering soul that is a poem, in all its unbecoming and rebirths, in all its falling apart and coming together again. 'How is it we heal?' she asks, this question a sort of thesis here, and then answers with the very book itself — for in it, in all its blooming ruin, we do."

—Alexander Shalom Joseph, Author of *The Clearing*

"Ashley Howell Bunn picks up 'small pieces of survival,' demonstrating that rebirth is possible even when we are sure collapse is irreparable. These poems, arising from the unbearable, find their way to 'sustenance/in abandon.' Using erasure as both form and concept, this poet makes clear that loss can be a form of discovery—in the aftermath of death, life surges into new embodiment and eros. We so badly need poems that have this kind of alchemical courage! *burning, breaking, building* offers grit and compassion in a time of universal upheaval. To read this book is to experience how absence breaks open to presence and 'heaves [us] into newness.'"

—Elizabeth Robinson, Author of *Vulnerability Index*

"A sober witness to the beat driven soul negotiating with the world. Ashley's terrain-driven use of language leaves you thirsty for more and staring up at the stars. Their poems will have you holding tight to your perceptions while gaining the courage to explore the inner depths. Hold open this book, take a deep breath, and dive into the deep water. It'll be worth going under."

—Ted Vaca, National Poetry Slam Champion & Coach

"*burning, breaking, building* is a powerful collection that upon flipping through and seeing the melting haibuns, erasures, and unconventional forms scattered throughout I thought it might be hiding something. In actuality, Ashley Howell Bunn is brave, vulnerable, and shattering in her brutal honesty and openness. I was taken on a revealing and relatable cyclical journey through recovery, familial relationships, aging, politics, love, and nature that left a burning behind my eyes—a sensation I've only felt by looking in the mirror when I wasn't ready to face myself. Bunn's ability to seamlessly sew these themes together with a balance of brashness and softness, while weaving syntax and sentiment has singed my brain. Yes, there's grief but the peaks of playfulness shine like stars on a quiet night—my heart was broken and pieced back together through wrenching specifics, begging the question, " How many times can I well up with tears to only turn the page and find relief bursting through?" *burning, breaking, building* will leave you in a state of dreamcore. You'll finish this collection with a deep, deep breath and want to turn back to page one for another read."

-Marissa Forbes, Author of *Surviving Peter Pan*

burning
breaking
building

ashley howell bunn

SOUTH BROADWAY PRESS
DENVER CO USA

Table of Contents

1 *drift*

2 *90 in 90*

5 *bread in the air*

6 *I'm in my late thirties, and I heard that*

7 *the timeline I didn't make it*

9 *Ojo Caliente*

10 *my sponsor tells me to ho out*

11 *old friend,*

12 *moon milk sweat*

14 *my right elbow*

15 *on my drive to work*

16 *spread open*

19 *cicada arcana*

22 *celestials: or what we give the dead*

24 *delicate skin*

25 *or*

26 *26 weeks*

28 *yin interrupted*

29 *early morning, election day*

32 *vision*

33 *it's the apocalypse, maybe we should fuck?*

34 *ember*

35 *I ask my six year old:*

36 *solstice*

37 *my star*

44 *how to drive home in the snow*

46 *what sober people do*

47 *depression hits*

48 *8 is some sort of infinity*

49 *at once*

50 *gratitude list on the eve of the Fall Equinox:*

51 *a bridge collapses and there is a poem about a thread breaking*

54 *something like virginia*

55 *I can't write a poem about your obituary*

56 *naïve melody (with the Talking Heads)*

58 *diagnosis*

59 *ivy*

62 *dreamcore*

63 *climate haven*

64 *resentments*

65 *summer november*

67 *and it, the sky*

68 *to the cabin*

70 *let it be known*

71 *casita*

72 *home*

73 *melt*

74 *on the anniversary of your death*

75 *acorn as areola*

preface

This collection investigates the connection of the universal and the temporal as we see it in fractals—repetitions in our lives and our selves and in the collective. The poems in this collection address how, with each cycle, we can reform, reframe, and be reborn. Through playing with the structure of the burning haibun, I explore my own cycles of parenthood, recovery, and grief. How what is no longer seen still resonates within us, getting to the heart of tenderness that connects us all.

Just like the repetition in a poem, life repeats its patterns. Dreams show us connections, the universe cycles itself through the mundane and profound. The patterns and repetitions we see in nature occur within us too. Yes, we are nature. We are natural, as much as we sometimes separate ourselves. Each leaf on the fern is similar and new. The repetition changes slightly with each bud. This idea of fractals is what started this book.

After I had my second child, I was struck by how so much of new motherhood was similar, yet entirely different. During my journey of recovery from substance abuse, the cycles of resentments, amends, pain and healing repeated, and with each cycle, brought a new birth. The circle of grief that surrounded me after the passing of my father brought a destruction and a renewal of self.

Each death is a birth. I have come to believe in multiple lifetimes, reincarnation. or multiple dimensions. Whatever eternity holds. I know that this is it. This is the place in which we start and end. There is just a journey, a compass, a crop-circle, a ripple in the waters of time that we inhabit, and then return to the depths. Only to return again.

—Ashley Howell Bunn

for Arlo,

my guiding star

drift

My sister scrubs the toilet until it full-moon shines
in the dark,
holds my mother's burdens like my father held a
drink.

When I was three months sober,
I spread his ashes in the woods outside my rehab.

A gray wave in the snow.
I've never liked the ocean.

Walking the beach by my father's home,
I stepped on a jellyfish, bulbous and soft,

like my mucus plug dropped
on the floor before labor.

Now, the winter has gone and the wildflowers
are probably swaying in some gentle breeze,

and my sister cleans the carpet desperately,
like I used to hold a drink,

and we pretend
we are different
from our parents.

90 in 90

I woke up to my partner's arm reaching to the back of the car *you found me I can't believe you found me* not once but twice passed out in the back seat my son cried he thought I was dead a man in treatment called himself a grateful alcoholic rivers on his arms he crawled outside after three days unconscious a vision of his daughter decided to live he lost his medical license now sits in quiet days listening to other people cry back hunched permanently pulling himself across the yard torso somehow dismembered from soul as if soul is only left in our limbs when we finally land that is why our hands shake my friend laughed like a sailor and had *nice stems for an old chick* a force of nature at the end of her story sobbed how she hated this disease hated how it gripped her choked her still I like morning coffee the beginning is somehow brighter the sunset brings the thought of another night my beautiful friend held me one evening as I broke into her bare breasts later she went to a shelter asked me for money I could've given her more watched my friends relapse in real time before their next drink the morning we were all asked to leave the virus is bigger than all of us our broken ness 90 meetings in 90 days I have missed 4 in a week but I am still sober there is a point to this sunrise coffee and drugged night's sleep trazodone clonidine hydroxyzine gabapentin post acute withdrawal can last for two years *grateful alcoholic* reading the AA words of the day laughing sober late into the night trauma re-emerging without anesthetic each morning walking out to look at the moon waiting for my gaze before its rest the stars would still be out cliché to begin or end with stars healing itself might be cliché to write still I like to end with stars

I woke up
not once but twice
alcoholic rivers
a vision of his daughter
now sits in quiet
permanently
dismembered from soul
that is why
our hands shake
a force of nature
this
disease I
like morning coffee
the sunset brings another
night
relapse
virus
broken ness
I am still sober
sunrise
grateful alcoholic
re-emerging
moon
end with stars

dismembered from soul
sunset brings another night
virus moon end stars

bread in the air

the greatest thing about dishes in the sink is that we have dishes and we have a sink and that I get to wash them when they get crusty and I hate that but there was food enough to be left behind and fungus enough in the air to make the dough rise and that you ate it with butter just like a victorian orphan and we laughed and then all played cards at the table and the greatest thing about the hole in the wall is that it is there and my hand made it and that there was emotion enough to propel it forward and that we are still here in this house and art sometimes covers the hole and sometimes it doesn't and one time you put your little shoe in the hole never to be seen again and I laughed and I found some old shoes to put on your feet and the best thing about that moment is that you have shoes and you have feet

I'm in my late thirties, and I heard that

itchy ears are a sign of perimenopause
as I sweat through the sheets
and lactate through my shirt

stick fingers and Q-tips in my
ear canal to try and soothe
what feels like a dry cavern,

a canyon, that hasn't seen
a river in millennia
as my hair falls in clumps

and my breasts swell and
sag like cycles of the moon,
which sounds beautiful but isn't,

because postpartum
and perimenopause
can happen at the same time

so can motherhood and
body dysmorphia, so can
feminism and misogyny

the timeline I didn't make it

There is a timeline in which I didn't make it.

I know this
because my astrologer told me
about at least one
where we loved each other so
much, it killed me.

An overdose.
Perhaps that's why
addiction is your greatest fear
in this life.

But I think there are more,
I feel it, as I hear about a mother
who didn't see her child grow.
Lost the battle, we like to say.

I know that is me
in some dimension.
I feel her kindred in
my bones, the heat in
my eyes, our stars connected

as I watch my sons play
on the floor. Miraculous to
exist here together on this
dirty carpet in this cluttered
room, in this beloved house.

As I drive my old neighborhood,
I get flashes of hands shaking, shooters
in purses and glove compartments to stop
them. Wondering how I can make it through
the day. Should I just crash the car?

Are these intrusive thoughts or just
memories unannounced? I wonder if the
guy at the liquor store thinks I died?

So what do I do with this Ashley
who is no longer here? With a son
left behind and one still in the
stars? The moment we split, when
I had the chance to live.

I know I'm lucky.
White girl with
straight teeth.
Insurance and enough
money for rehab.

I know where I would be.
My timelines collapse
and my Ashleys intertwine.
My children burst inside me
and spiral out to their own
universe, and I am still here.

They say our clay reforms together
each time, we have similar elements.
In this life, I think you told me I had
to get well. You pushed me there. But
we couldn't do it together. There's that one
song, we will both find out, just not together.

You are always the you in my poems.
I am always
talking to you.

Ojo Caliente

was there moon
or satellite reaching mounds of earth
into circus of breath and Eve
face to the sun
feet feeding
iron
pores quenching
lithium
rubbing arsenic
into our creases
moved heaving and slow
kisses gravel and dirt
dust and climax
wet unlike this ground
which somehow still
grows us

my sponsor tells me to ho out

You need to ho out, she tells
me. Let yourself get messy.
Let yourself get hurt
by a woman. Even if it reminds
you of your mother. You date too
many men who remind you of
your father. What is it that you
want? Can you be alone? Can you
leave the next morning? Don't leave
a number. Let your body
want, and know it is good.
Let that soft animal love.

old friend,

it's these colorado days
with snow on the ground
but warmth in the air
four pm and the sky is darkening pink
we would walk
along our muddy path
to where
the trees covered us
then we would sigh
open ourselves
to the space between us
allow our molecules to merge
as we walked
and talked of our love
our spouses
our children
past lives and current
how we've always known

I smell the air today
years after our early winter walks
gaze towards the
mountains
send a wave across the ocean of my city
and let myself break towards you

moon milk sweat

I made some moon water
in the taurus full moon,
beaver moon, mourning moon.
It repeats each year, the cycle.

I repeat, too; we do.

The first time I gave birth, numb from waist
down, frantic and exhausted.
So was my child, covered in ash
when he emerged, like he had
already been through battle.

My milk was translucent, as it
waited in bags to be consumed,
like me.

There are states that stress leaves
the body, ways our nervous system
reacts.

The night sweats are common
in both postpartum and withdrawal.
So is terror.

Sometimes, in memory, it is hard
to tell if I was hormonal, or dying,
or both.

In dreams, I am often lucid.
Which I hate. I want the predictability of
this plane. The worst is when
I think I'm awake, and then something
changes, just slightly, and I know
I'm not.

The clock doesn't have numbers,
I can't read my phone, the couch
is misplaced, there is a random
bowl of peas on the floor.
Reality is a precarious thing.

Once, when I was trying to
sweat the alcohol out
of my system, I woke in
my dream and decided to
fly. *Fuck it,* I thought, and
left through the window.

Over houses and land, oceans.
Touching the water gently before
gliding upward. Upward. Stars
and stars. And stars until no more
stars and I knew if I kept going, I
wouldn't come back. I thought about
it. For a long time. Decided to return
for my son, asleep in the next room.

The second time I gave birth
I could feel
it all.

my right elbow

hurts when I pick things up
or reach above my head,

a reminder of how
I hurt you.

You grabbed my arm,
as I tried to leave,
pulled me back in
over and over.

The person in addiction
is always in the wrong,
right?

Three years sober and I
still can't pick up my
morning coffee without
flinching. How is it
that we heal?

on my drive to work

I saw a woman with a Joni Mitchell braid and
beret.
I imagined she was walking, skates in hand,
to her river on this cold December morning,

and when that song came on, the one that always
makes my eyes see far back in time with you, the
geese
in the park all took flight at once, hundreds in
their
magic dance on this cool December morning,

but I forgot, again, to get cash from the bank,
so I could give some to the man who always
works the corner I turn on from Colorado Blvd,
so when I stopped I had to wave him off again,
ashamed,
but he still smiled at me on this warm December
morning,

and there is still grace and love and music
and magic in the world,
even when we know the what's coming is hard,
because:
the people are rising
and breathing,
we are singing, and
the geese are flying,
I am still loving you, and
Joni is still skating away.

spread open

The woman on the plane next to me, baby on her lap, is crying. She was crying on the tarmac, with a man with red hair. Now she is on the plane alone with her child, holding the child close, tears still falling. Once the baby falls asleep she starts looking through pictures of her and the man and the baby, all smiling, zooming in on the man's face, the man in the water, zooming in on the back of his legs, the baby dancing at a wedding, zooming in on the man's smile, the baby's dress. All of them smiling on a green mountain, zooms in on the baby's hat, the man's sweaty smile, his hand resting around her waist. She doesn't know I'm watching from across the aisle, she doesn't feel my eye hold her baby's red hair, how it reminds me of a Sylvia Plath poem, glowing in the sun, the look on her face. I know I shouldn't be part of this moment, but I am. Her bare shoulders and the hairs on them illuminated through the light of the oval window, she must be chilly, the hairs on her arms perk up slightly, her hair catching the breeze of the overhead vent, her child gumming her chest as she sleeps. These moments are what make a life
so I let myself fall in love

The woman
crying. a
man with red hair.
holding the child close

pictures
man
in the water his legs,
baby dancing the
man's smile
a green mountain
resting around her
waist.
her baby's red
hair Sylvia Plath
glowing in the sun,
I am. Her
bare shoulders illuminated
oval
the hairs on her arms her
hair catching
her chest as she sleeps. These
moments are what make a life so I let myself
in love

spread open crying
green mountain around her waist
the hairs on her arms

her baby's red hair
a man glowing in the sun
illuminated

These moments in love
I am. Her bare shoulders
her chest as she sleeps

I don't know if it is poetry to hold you until you feel safe, but here is my heartbeat

I don't know how to write the body into verse, but here is my hand

I don't know if *The Paris Review* will publish my body next to yours, but here is my pulse

I don't know if I can write you an exhale, but here is my inhale

I don't know how to metaphor the tension from your jawline, but here is my chest

I don't know the syntactical breaks in your heart, but here is my thumb in the curve of your back, the arch of your foot, the soft space behind your knee

I don't know if I can write you into ease, into a body that is no longer in pain, into a place where you can truly rest, into a world that no longer threatens. I don't know if I can write you into a mother's arms which hold you like you should have been held, into a childhood with laughter and generosity, into true joy. I don't know what it is to heal a person, but here I am, with you. I am here with you, but here is all of me.

cicada arcana

wingless cicadas
waiting seventeen years to
be born into light

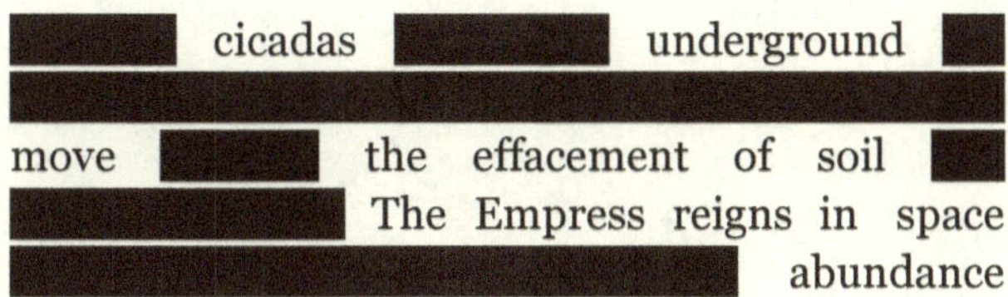

wingless cicadas are active underground the
decomposition of sap tells them when to
move through the effacement of soil and
earth my father The Empress reigns in space
outside of lack now lives in abundance

anniversary
of my father's death I pulled
the Empress, for him

buried baby waits
before their emergence
wings
singing, a chance to
grow his roots

to show a man
the world stops

like the buried cicadas my baby waits for
seventeen years before their emergence
wings bursting for their last moments
leaves, light, singing, climaxing a chance to
grow his roots again in nitrogen I check my
underwear for signs of labor some bloody
show to show no one but when a man bleeds
the world stops

waiting for labor
perineal massage and
bursts of blood and stars

only my cervix keeps us whole stars created by stars before them I need to let him rest this periphery of sun and leaves we all begin again exhale a death inhale a crowning an empress the cicadas are coming this year

celestials: or what we give the dead

my friend said she bought me a kaleidoscope
the week you woke me in a dream,
to show me the fullness of
                    the moon
        framed   in my window

startled me out of night, like the sun
disappearing the stars with its life,

obsidian, the sky, I imagine,
before I woke,
which is supposed
to keep excited souls from waking
the still living on a sunday before sunrise

so I place it next to your altar

the man who does magic with the
mesa told us to say goodnight
to our dead before we rest or fuck
or drink ourselves retching cover
with cloth close a door tuck them
in so they don't watch the depth of
living are you still dying or are you
done now father

collect objects
to make you comfortable:
magnolia pod,
driftwood,
carolina pine,
an image of your young body,
your silver hair,
your burnt bones,

I do not place the shot of vodka
I was going to drink in your honor.
I pour it to the earth,
give my sobriety.

delicate skin

I observe my mother-in-law sitting at the dining room table, she wipes my father-in-law's face gently with a napkin, moving the cloth around, tucking in each crumb left behind from lunch, cradling his jaw as he opens his mouth, singing to him as she brushes his teeth, takes the electric razor, humming, to his cheeks and chin and neck, delicate hanging skin, rubbing his shoulder as she shaves under his nose with one hand. He coos and grunts, the only words he shares now, she smiles and keeps singing, says:

thank you,

sweetie, as she finishes.

Thank you for letting me take care of you.

or

I carry you with me
like a memory, or a skin tag,
or that feeling when you find the
perfect word in your line,
or leave a perfect space

on the page.
The same feeling as seeing a mountain sunset,
somewhere in your belly-chest,
a heavy joy that tears your eyes,
like holding your child,
or remembering you are mortal
at 3 am on a Tuesday.
Something about the eternal and the temporal.
Something about beauty and love.

I watched my dog as he was dying,
out on the porch,
eyes closed and soft,
face to the sun.

26 weeks

we will see it all
she whispers
as she pushes into my side
pressing flesh between fingers and wand
everything looks great

your femur appears from
the watery ink

Pause
click

prints an image for us to hold

how's the pressure
I can't decide if she means on my belly
or in my heart
as the air I breathe moves to your blood
you emerge sideways
ghostlike from my bloody shore

here's the aortic arch
she speaks to her student
who I have allowed in the room
to view all that I hold inside

look at those ovaries, beautiful
I see only shadows
sunken faces

then

your profile: elf-like, angelic
sagittal view
split in half

like when you arrived
like every moment since
split between two selves

the wand moves again
and you sink
into black water

yin interrupted

body lying prone
chin
resting on a block
small child
curled to my
side

the
back
of his
head,
matted
locks
he
refuses
to
brush
out

the corners of my mat
hold
us

our
lines
perforate
together
and
apart as
our
air
finds
each
other

our lines perforate together and apart as our air
finds each other

early morning, election day

my baby wakes me early on election day. I have voted, again, and the sky is pink. I can see it through the skylight in my living room. The leaves have already fallen on the tree peeking through, and the branches make art patterns on this sky canvas. My morning pages consist of a poem about questions and on-the-spot Tonglen. Both very important things to remember on a day like any day, but especially a day like today. I am the blue morning, the poet says, so I am this pink morning. I am new and somewhat hopeful, and mostly despair. I breathe it in for my neighbor and friend, breathe out what little peace I can muster, try to send some pink sky across the city streets—which are beautifully quiet at this early hour—only just beginning to stir. I send it into their chest, through their sternum, into their lungs and branches, little bulbs of floating air, bronchi and bronchioles, alveolus and alveoli, a spell, an italian menu whispered in the candlelight, air moving into the deepest part of their cavern, the diaphragmatic surface, let their body push it out for the next person, as we wake into whatever this new day might hold.

I have
voted, again, the sky is pink.
in my living room.

this
canvas.
on-the-spot Tonglen.

a day like today.
I am this pink morning.
and mostly despair.
breathe
out what little peace
city streets

chest,
sternum, lungs branches,
bulbs bronchi bronchioles,
alveolus alveoli, a spell,
whispered air
diaphragmatic

we wake

I voted again
so I am this pink morning
diaphragmatic

vision

this picture
picture this

can you say my name
shh ash ahsh ash

show me the writing
on the wall
we are where

where are we
hos spit al spit
hos pit all
whose spit

spit it out
hospice in sit
respite in
a word be might
hospite

hold it
like my name
ash

it's the apocalypse, maybe we should fuck?

By fuck, I mean that I thought of you while driving
through the plains.
The wind pushed so hard it stagnated the birds in
their flight

and I thought about the desert and what the sun
would feel like
and what you would feel like on me

but I think you like the cold and I could see purple
mountains
and blue snow out the window as we drove

those nights when the sky is so bright it almost
ceases to exist
like when thighs open and there is an end but not
really and we keep coming

back to when I'd like to meet you here again but
this is the end of something
and the sand and snow of other lifetimes mixes with
my clay

and we reform, again
and again,

all I'm saying is that if this is the end where is our
climax

and I want to spread open and open and open until
I cease to exist

ember

my friend holds ash and salt in his mouth while he reads, rolls it with his tongue and swallows like it could be nourishment, and as I write I think of all that's left after fire or drought, grains of grief and electricity, and when I gave birth the burning is what I remember most and my legs which would not be part of me, and the ember in the middle of my torso, loosened and emerged a smallness covered in off-white vernix like wet ash and my body and his are not part of this place that we have been pushed into and as my blood left me and dried on the floor those crystals glowing orange in the hospital light

I ask my six-year-old:

What were you before you were here?

Maybe some grass I think? I like grass.

What will you be after?

I heard heaven is the best you could have
so I think it would be three million trees I could run
through

We notice together:

Backs against the ground, pink smoke and red sun,
we can't see the meteor shower because the world
is on fire but he says

these clouds are nice

and

the stars still matter even
if we can't see them

solstice

I prefer the dark;
I love when the sky dims at 4 pm.
No obligation for movement or progress,
only firelight and
cocooning into this small nest
we have created together.

As the light returns, slowly,
I'll take the last of the darkness
piece by piece,

into my pockets and ear canals,
my womb and shoes,
to keep with me as
the world opens
its terrible
eye.

my star

my son's world a kaleidoscope and many refuse to look with him when he was four I trusted other people to hold him and guide him but they pulled him by the roots and let them dry out on the hot concrete

on the hot concrete I found him and took him back
to the sweetness of the soil in our small garden so
he would have some chance to drink our tears and
leave the salt behind in small crystalline mountains

crystalline mountains in the distance and the sun
shines through an ember to keep the fire in the
stove alive as the snow falls not like ash

like ash there was a grayness blanketing his
microcosm of thin hair and skin translucent a liquid
coursing through wound and then placenta like
paper and pulp

pulp remnants of sound uttered in darkness or
screamed in fluorescent vowels declared since the
beginning of mouths and larynx

larynx of the first cry the first air after fluid home
and cosmos held in eyes waiting for vibration

vibration expansion spirit through flesh at this
point of awareness

how to drive home in the snow

make sure
it is night
and look up
preferably next to a street lamp
see each flake falling
as if just for this moment

onto your sister's shoulder
rest your fingers there also
gently
her breath catching in the
cold
then her chest
breaking

later
you will sit in the driveway
notice it stopped snowing
walk inside
start again
with what's left

now
let her stand still
in the parking lot
let yourself too
as long as you both
can stand the cold

eventually
make your way to the car
brush crystals from the windshield
examine their shards in the light
of that streetlamp
you
hopefully
found

drive away from the hospital
slowly
notice
the lights in the trees
your hands on the wheel
your struggle to connect them
to your body

then
back to luminescence
your father
gazing out the window
amazed
at all
he had missed

be careful

as you remember
holding his hand
stroking his hair
the glow of the monitors

what sober people do

fuck in the back of a car

next to the expensive house,
next to the expensive espresso

the jogger dads rush manicured children past,
you try to cover your bare ass with a blanket

the wife comes out to water the lawn,
the forecast calls for snow

she glares as you drive away laughing,
to say goodbye on the next corner,
kiss through the window
move into evening light

wanting a cigarette to end the moment,
craving body and liquid

still craving the relief of sadness

depression hits

after retching all night and half a day
a virus rather than drink this time
yes, it's been eighteen months
and
today I remembered what it felt like
to sweat through the sheets
and give away my remains to the half-filled bin
to want oblivion so much
it hurts to wake
like when I googled
heft only to find rot
while trying to write
a poem about my breasts
what lies underneath their
heart, rot which affects beets
imagine their dirty heartbeats
and bleeding skin under the
surface of the ground, as I try
to pull myself out of the covers
walk downstairs to find the mess
on another day I might find gratitude in
dishes in the sink and his small
clothes scattered in piles around the house
the dog hair in the carpet and what the fuck is
that stain on the couch—
morning heaviness
morning heft
I heave myself into newness
hoping I come back tomorrow
hoping this rot hasn't yet reached my heart

8 is some sort of infinity

I think of you and your soft and swollen fingers and how I still want to hold them as you suffer and cry and there are so many parts to you which swell and crack and you told me as we met in the dream realm that you have hurt for so long I think you were never fully whole and I said I was sorry but that maybe you could feel better for a few days before you leave and congestive heart failure is something I know of but the percentages I don't understand like eight percent of your heart is working and is this basically time to say goodbye and that eight percent I would like to say goodbye to and forgive in some way and I'm sorry only eight percent of your heart is here to say goodbye but I think that

and my heart a phantom limb feels like it is also failing and when I breathe in my chest aches and my fingers shake like I know yours are as you try to sign the paper to be released and on the phone you said this is the end and I said it was the end long ago and I could hear your breaking and can't tell if it is also mine

there are so many things I have written to you in the last few months when you chose drowning instead of life and now you call and say you love me and I believe it even though I can't understand how you could do those things but here we are and I wanted you to die last week to not have to grieve a walking corpse but since eight percent of you is here to say goodbye just know that I hope in the next life you are my child so I can give you roots and so you can grow and I hope I am not the parent you were to me and I hope for that the ninety-two percent of you that was forgotten

at once

my therapist once told me we can hold
two truths at once
my body made a body gave life and gives life
and is a heavy suit I can't escape I am grateful
I am imprisoned
if my childhood friend had kissed me and let me
hold her tiny hand
I might have never touched a boy and
I love my partner and his big bear paws
holding our son

it is possible to know the body
and love the body to not
recognize the body
to hate the body
and be amazed at each cell
to be in awe and fear of each curve

I want to be a man
no, I want to be a glowing orb

to remember we all are the stars in space
and blood
the light breaking through the cracks the
ferns in the canyons
the lines in hands and around eyes the specs of
quartz in the granite
the energy from root to crown masculine and
feminine
embodied and eternal at once

gratitude list on the eve of the fall equinox:

gold leaves and the cracks behind my front bottom teeth I can run my tongue along when I am nervous and warm coffee on cold mornings and that line between my eyebrows I know means I have done a lot of thinking and pink sunrises and sunsets and the way my friend pulls at the rings on her fingers when she is nervous and words on pages and words sticky on tongues and bursting out of throats

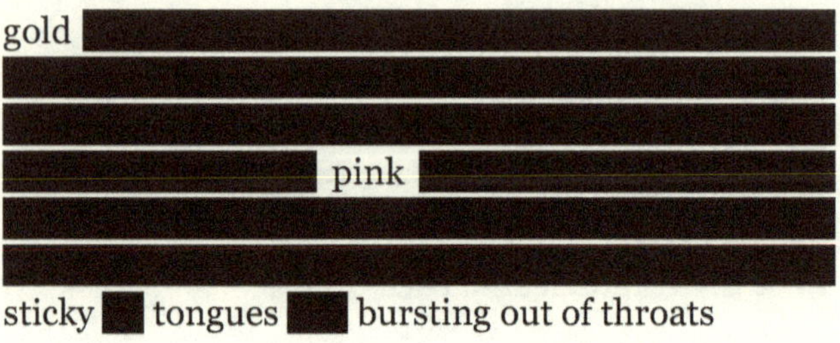

pink sunrises
sticky
bursting out of throats

a bridge collapses and there is a poem about a thread breaking

*

three flights for life and two car crashes later
I am on the phone with my sister
while the nurse puts the screen to my father's slant
jaw
fogged eyes
says she is busy
can't hold it up to his silence forever
my sister and I discuss
how we want to be buried
in the roots of a tree
or thick fungus
at least he said goodbye
before his dissection
colon and heart and brain
fluid and feces
what it is that makes a body

*

and I keep trying to write about my father but the
sway of another summer grass hits my skin and I
find myself imagining this distant lover hears my
shoes click in the halls of the hospital an echo
makes his head turn and think of me with the band
playing and the pub overflowing with some kind of
joy as we ate chips and vinegar in the alley and
laughed too hard for too long before my dream and
that poem and the car crash branding my arm
he said it wouldn't leave a scar

*

I walk my selfishness
through fluorescence
disinfectant
regimes

burning white
prone bodies breathing machinery
piston lungs
ribcages creak and broaden
each rotation
brambles breaking
in flaming tinder
the bodies are held by none
and the heat of summer fires
lies dormant
but waiting
the virus keeps dancing
with our ghosts
like zephyr

*

and my lover purred, whirred, handed me a folded
poem about a thread breaking about time and
distance and cliché about scaffolding and bridges
holding and I dreamed his gentle vastness buried
his eyes the same sad as the day he ran out the door
to wave goodbye as I drove away with hair in his
face and plaid shirt sagging   I slammed on the
brakes

*

the world burns and my father dies
friends fear for their lives in streets
lungs and skin
what is it that makes a body
at least he said sorry
before his dismemberment
when the flesh is failing
love comes through the curve of a lip

a groan
sigh
twitch of a finger
a knowing
whisper visible in cold

*

it begins to snow outside the hospital window
when my father could still speak
he called to it

something like virginia

I burned the spider's web
with the match for my candle
soft smoke rising
as I turned back to my other tasks
small pieces of survival
accounts and numbers, hair on the carpet,
coins for the laundry

later
lying on the couch
weary from a day I can't remember
saw her silhouette moving
to rebuild in the middle of the night
glow from our apartment courtyard
backlight her delicacy
her tenderness
her spiny limbs and
crushable bulb heart
I so admired her strength

I need to clean the pot of soup we had for dinner,
the dishes in the sink, the boy needs lunch
tomorrow, there are words waiting for reply always
hovering just above

feeling the need to dust
wipe her life into my cloth again
instead,
I welcome her home
let myself rest

I can't write a poem or your obituary

Can't remember the transition of body to static or
hair before silver, skin before wax

Can't remember the last thing you said to me or
the last time you made me laugh, last time you
made me cry

Can't remember how to make metaphor out of
melancholy or what melancholy was before this

Can't remember when I realized death or
that you would also die

Can't remember being five or
having my head on your chest,
can't remember heartbeat

Can't remember what heartbeat symbolizes or
how to write its rhythm into verse

Can't remember what stories we wrapped around as
you shifted or what smile was before slack

Can't remember if you believed in heaven but
I think you knew hell

Remember your eyes up and to the right, but
couldn't see what held you,
couldn't see what you followed as you left.

naïve melody (with Talking Heads)

Did I find you or you find me?

I've summoned you many times before

Eyes that light up

On the night sky trail

Home is where I want to be

Running down the hill with your red track pants

I note the passing of time

I sent you a letter on grief the day your father passed

The less we know about it the better

Those old love notes, friend notes, I rose in love, fellow traveler, soul-friend, Anam Cara, keep your stars out

There was a time before we were born

I wrote you a poem called *fuck Cathy and Heathcliff*, about hitting our ghosts with my car

You've got light in your eyes

And I wrote a poem about your wife, about how I wonder what she sounds like in her tenderness, her openness

Make it up as we go along

I wrote you a poem about my skin tag and the Costco parking lot, and how it felt like you were choking me

Someone said this is where I'll be

I wrote you a poem about stars

I'll love you til my heart stops

I gifted you those stars

Sing into my mouth

You gifted me some expansion of fidelity you couldn't keep

You've got a face with a view

I summoned you to the city streets of Dublin

To the skyline of London

This Colorado creekside

Love you til I'm dead

But I guess I'm already there

diagnosis

All of this is overwhelming but maybe

Doubling down on meds will

Help

Didn't the moon look beautiful last night?

ivy

the ivy I bought at the witchcraft store that reminded me of my father because it reminded him of north carolina, and he loved north carolina, is dying. I don't know what I did wrong, the person who was wearing all black but made it look cool and not scary told me that it was easy to take care of, and I put it by the window that gets sun but not too much sun and when I wear all black I feel like I just look depressed. I didn't even wear all black to my father's funeral because he didn't even really have a funeral because it was canceled because my stepmother got covid so I guess I didn't even have a chance to wear all black and I think I need to repot it. maybe if I get a bigger pot the roots will have more space or think they are outside and grow. the ivy my dad remembered in north carolina would climb walls and up trees but this ivy I just wanted to kind of cascade down the table by his picture. but it is dying and he is dead and when I finally spread his ashes I don't remember what color I was wearing.

the ivy
is
dying. I did wrong,
all black
it was easy
by the window
my
father's funeral
was canceled
all black
bigger roots
more space and grow
my dad would
climb up trees I just wanted to
cascade by his
dying
I don't remember what color

and it was easy
I just wanted to cascade
I don't remember

dreamcore

My son told me about the word dreamcore,
that he was nostalgic for places he had never
known.
I asked him if he meant like castles or magical
forests.
He said no, like 90s office buildings,
like with telephones that are attached to the walls
and brown carpets and really slow elevators.
He said, *when I think about fax machines,*
my heart hurts because it's like I knew them
at one point, and now I don't and I miss them.

I don't know what to say to this, as I continue to
drive down I-25 on the way home from school.
I have never know the moors of Ireland
but find myself longing for them,
I have never known the depths of the
Appalachian woods, but my heart hurts for them.
These seem like appropriate places to miss.

Then, I think,
I have never known true poverty, true hunger,
have never known losing a child
or bleeding out in childbirth.
So I let go of my judgment for my child's longing for
what must seem like simpler days,
of phone lines and fax machines,
days before cell phones and social media, of likes
and follows,
and we finish our drive, letting
Dreamcore rest in our subtle bodies, as we make
our way home.

climate haven

an elegy for Asheville

My sister and I always joked
that when the climate apocalypse came,
at least we had the land our family
left us outside of Asheville.

We had to sell the cabin,
because we couldn't afford the taxes,

but we had that last tree-lined ridge,
with the view of Grandfather Mountain,
Tanawha, Great Eagle, Great Hawk,
next to the creek, with plenty of rich soil,
and a long growing season.

We could always take our kids and meet there,
let them run through the white and yellow pines,
catch crawdads, no need for shoes
when there is moss to hold feet.

Where is that ridge now?
I imagine it under water or mud.
Land drowning in itself.

"There is no Safe Place," the headlines read
as the people grieve their mountain haven
and sift through what's left.

My family underwater,
my grandparents'
floating in their graves.

There is no safety here, child
they cry
there is no safe place

resentments

I go through my resentments at the end of the day
not wanting to look at the one I know I must.
He calls for me to come tuck him in.
I put away the note from school.
Another hard day, another meltdown.
Take a long breath, notice the length of my exhale,
the cadence, the texture, like the bottom of my shoe,
smell the coffee sitting cold on the counter
from the morning, the old dishes in the sink,
hear the clank as he drops his water bottle upstairs,
my heart quickens,
eyes burn, move my attention to my heart,
some knot to untangle, I'll have to save that for
later, after the kids are both in bed,
force myself upstairs and heave my body
next to his on the
messy bed, glue sticks and fabric,
pokemon cards and scraps of
paper fall to the floor as we press together, his soft
animal melts into mine
as I place my hand on his heart, and ask him what
he needs to calm down,
just cuddles, he says.
I listen to his breath—slow, notice the cadence, the
texture, like soft cotton, the whir of the fan, the
warmth of his chest, as we untangle our knots
together.

summer   november

they are mowing the grass in november
and the roly poly I almost killed underfoot
stays on course
dear friend   how are we still here

and
I think

about going
down on him
while he reads poetry
the crack   in his voice merging
with his river
crescendo and   caesura
rise   and   slow
with each stanza

and today   I walked the creek
with my friend
watched   the children
leaves in wind
no snow yet   and we discuss the coming
fires

and
I think

about him   inside me
distract myself from   the
uncovering
salt   to wash   my words
because   what   words   do   I
have   once the muscle
relaxes
around   cancerous jaws
syllables masticated

and
I think

about that small creature
moving   through
summer november

where is it going
and
does it   care

and it, the sky,

after Alexander Shalom Joseph

contrasts against the yellow leaves
leaking milk and honey
over dry, paper plains

pulls dark lavender
from behind the mountains

pushes breath from stars
into lungs, tells us to
inhale, allows us

and it, the sky,
did not weep on us today,
even though we could feel it,

the tension

of mourning, yet to be released

to the cabin

your door was locked
I made do on your deck
rust red old boards sighing underfoot

I'm not sure when you were painted
when you were even built

so much needed fixing
my father was not a handyman

he knew you in freckles and term papers
drinking before it became drunkenness
marriage before it became divorce

I wanted so badly to see
his fingerprint in your paint
some part of him here with me

part of you

but I felt him more in the wet air and land
on which you rest
I found your address
and drove an hour out of Asheville
to gaze through your window at the coffee mugs
still on the table

I always say I don't want to die in the desert
where everything dries out and stays

I'd rather die somewhere like here
and let the moss melt me away

I turn to watch the wind move the mountains
and a curtain of rain over the hills

almost two years since he left

I want to buy this land
repaint your deck
press my thumb into the paint as it dries

sit outside just like this
watch the Carolina rain
let my father's ashes rest beside my coffee
in the morning light

trace my father's path
on your dusty floors

let it be known

that I moved out and the bed is in the same place and fog rests and plants are and that there is water falling and my hands are flesh and joints and plastic veins let it be known that the kitchen door doesn't close all the way but the bathroom door slams shut that sunflowers move and the mountains were once glass beach

water in my hands
and sunflowers move mountains
veins in place of fog

casita

there are ten trees
to hold our weight
like the
six
strings
tied
from your fingers
to
my
waist

home

I want to cut my hair
bake it into a pie
feed you

until you
come

there is sustenance
in abandon

he left

a canyon road
smoking cigarette
mountaintop

melt

it falls apart we all got ***work to do*** the radio says, **I listen to** the song again until the dopamine is sucked out of it, **the mountains** are visible today, the smoke from california has dissipated and **the air** smells like **melting snow** so I **roll down the window** and let myself **remember** taking walks after work with you, **let**ting the snow and **mud soak our feet** as we talked, the cops **spring** down the street and I read that one of the **ICE** raids happened right on the corner by my house, they took **a woman and infant** in their bus and where did they go, did the protest on Wednesday do anything and I'm glad that **the wind died down and the sun** is still out at least a little when I leave work now, it gets dark ***we all got work to do*** is in the song I **keep listening** to on repeat, my brain needs repetition to **feel safe** and I forgot to get cash so I can give it to the guy who washed my windshield on Colorado Blvd. so I try to give him an old Starbucks gift card and he just **smile**s **and say**s no worries, **the sun just** set and the headlights hurt my eyes **driving home**

all got work to do
melting snow and ice and sun
woman and infant

on the anniversary of your death

It's January,
and I'm wearing the sweater
from the day you died.

Buying it, I knew
I would hold your hand
wearing it as you left me.

acorn as areola

he roots on my right breast
hungry and wanting

I know the milk is coming
electricity trickles through fat and lymph

compasses my areola
drips into my bra

a crop circle in the cotton
seen from space

patterns communicating
what is already in us

mountains melting to
papillary ridges

annual rings
echoing

> when I was a child, I would climb trees
> speak to the fairies living in the bark
> imagine I was an Irish peasant with a tan
> apron an English servant walking the moors
> always servitude and magic

now, I wipe halos into the kitchen counters
breathe fractals into the early morning air

contractions (a strawberry burst)
pain and joy as he crowned

and sunlight
there is that

as an acorn holds the whole of the tree
sprout to decay

he moves to the left breast
roots
and eats

"To erase—within the realm of poetry—any text, even a self-authored text, is a political act."

—torin a. greathouse

Writing from the Ashes: On the Burning Haibun
On the generative failures within a text.
By torrin a. greathouse
Originally Published: July 02, 2023

Poetry Foundation

ACKNOWLEDGEMENTS

“drift” and “90 in 90” are forthcoming with *Talon Review* – University of North Florida *Vol. 3 Issue 6, Fall 2025*

“cicada arcana” was published in another form in *Anti-heroin Chic*, Summer 2024

“acorn as areola,” “something like virginia,” and “depression hits” were previously published in Querencia Press *Not Ghosts but Spirits Volume 5, 2024*

“vision,” “8 is some sort of infinity,” “bread in the air,” “a bridge collapses and there is a poem about a thread breaking,” and “I can’t write a poem or your obituary” were previously published in *in coming light* by Middle Creek Publishing, 2022

“celestials: or what we give the dead” was previously published by Twenty Bellows, 2022

“Ojo Caliente” and “how to drive home in the snow” were previously published by *Champagne Room Journal,* Summer 2023 Issue 03

“it’s the apocalypse, maybe we should fuck?” was previously published by Global Poemic, 2021

“ember” was previously published by Mulberry Literary, 2021

“at once” was previously published in *We do not need Permission to Rise* by Beyond the Veil Press, 2025

“early morning, election day” was previously published in the *Embers* anthology by Twenty Bellows, 2025

ABOUT THE AUTHOR

Ashley Howell Bunn (she/they) completed her MFA in poetry through Regis University and holds a MA in Literature from Northwestern University. Their work has appeared in many places both in print and online. Their first chapbook, *in coming light*, was published in 2022 by Middle Creek Publishing and their second chapbook, *Living Amends*—coauthored with Alexander Shalom Joseph, will be available through Galileo Press in 2026. Their work has been supported by Bread Loaf Writers' Conference and Sundress Publications. She is an adjunct instructor of English at the Community College of Denver and the Youth Program Coordinator at Lighthouse Writers Workshop. She is a certified somatic coach and yoga guide, and she offers somatic writing workshops in-person and virtually. When she isn't writing, she is practicing yoga, running in the sunshine, playing with her kids, or daydreaming and staring off into space.

Author Photograph: © Marissa Morrow

ABOUT THE PRESS

South Broadway Press
is a publisher of poetry through books,
print journals, and on our online journal.

OUR MISSION

Our mission is to provide a platform through poetry, writing, and the arts for ideas that provide alternatives to the harmful systems and ideologies that we historically have and continue to live among. We are interested in work that points us towards symbiosis with not just other humans, but with all beings in this moment, all beings past, and those future beings that will be impacted by the choices we collectively, and individually, make today. We focus our attention on love as a guiding force. Not a love that only reactively supports those who have been afflicted by oppression, but a love that is willing to disrupt, disobey, and proactively prevent and redirect the potential forthcoming affliction around us. A love that is resolute in its boundaries for itself and others. A love that takes the form of dissent, resistance, and in the words of John Lewis, a love that is willing to "get into good trouble".

OUR SEAL

Our seal is **the Bear, the Wrench, and the Quill.**

The Bear as a symbol of balancing softness with strength. The Bear as a call to approaching the caves of our internal worlds with curiosity. To slow living, and to laying witness to ourselves as not just material beings walking this Earth, but celestial beings, such as the great bear that graces the winter sky above us.

The Wrench as a symbol of disruption. A willingness to throw a wrench into the gears of fascism.

The Quill as a reminder of the adage that "the pen is mightier than the sword", and a calling to approach our work and play with that integrity and power in mind.

Our seal is also a nod to **Mutiny Information Cafe**, a bookstore, coffee shop, and community hub for over ten years now. A space that has time and again proved home for the cultivation of revolutionary ideas and the soft hearts that hold them.

www.ingramcontent.com/pod-product-compliance
Lightning Source LLC
LaVergne TN
LVHW051015080826
845145LV00009B/2628

* 9 7 8 1 7 3 5 0 3 5 5 5 0 *